FACILITY MANAGEMENT AND OUTSOURCING RELATIONSHIP

KA LEUNG LOK & DAVID BALDRY

Made with ♥ on the Notion Press Platform
www.notionpress.com

Contents

Prologue

Table of content

CHAPTER ONE

Introduction

Although the construction industry has long been a powerful engine for Hong Kong's economic growth, the industry experienced a drastic reduction in workloads and a change in market structure following the Asian economic turmoil in 1997 (Chiang et al., 2013). Consequently, regional FM outsourcing services for built environments have grown more common. These outsourcing services include computer integrated FM, catering/vending, moving management, project management (for both major and minor works), services installation (i.e., mechanical, electrical) and cleaning or security services (Moore and Finch, 2004). In the late 1990s in Hong Kong, expenditures for in-house services became a greater burden with the drop in rental incomes, and building owners outsourced many of these services (Lai, Yik and Jones, 2008; Yik and Lai, 2005). To decrease their costs, many commercial building owners chose to outsource operations and maintenance work, according to the results of their feasibility studies. The Tertiary Education Facilities Management Association (2011) reports that more than 50% of its benchmark data are found in the facilities management services at the seven universities in Hong Kong, including energy consumption, maintenance services, refurbishments and building operating costs, and especially the costs of security services, cleaning and waste management services.

Kok, et al. (2011) find that cleaning and maintenance services have a major and direct effect on students' academic achievement, and that catering and security services can affect staff and student satisfaction and the organisation's image. These four facility services can each add specific values to the higher education sector. This study thus focuses on the four FM outsourcing services of maintenance, cleaning, security and catering, as they are supplied in Hong Kong's higher education sector.

Before discussing client and service provider relationships or the nature of their operational and management elements, it is important to distinguish between the two terms of 'contracting-out' and 'outsourcing'. 'Contracting-out' normally refers to those services that continue to be provided in-house but have been directly contracted, whereas 'outsourcing' refers to services that continue to be procured from external providers.

The purpose of this study is to investigate the outsourcing relationships between the clients and service providers in a key sector of Hong Kong's economy. Fully understanding these outsourcing relationships requires taking a holistic view of the fundamental elements of outsourcing, including the nature, services, strategies and the management of relationships. Such an understanding also involves examining these elements within appropriate theoretical models. The literature reveals the general working mechanisms of outsourcing (Boer et al., 2006; Maskell et al., 2005), but the significance of this study lies in its explication of the previously obscure relationships between FM outsourcing service providers and their clients.

In recent decades, integrated resource planning (the main resources being people, property and technology) has become an important part of FM. It is generally believed that the optimal use of high-quality facilities can solve business problems in the built and human environment. To operate such facilities, outsourcing is now prevalent in various industries. This procurement approach is considered by some proponents to be an effective and efficient approach to managing resources (Adegoke and Adegoke, 2013; Agndal and

Nordin, 2009; Hamzah et al., 2010; Ikediashi et al. 2013; Kadefors, 2008; Li and Choi, 2009). However, organisations often fail to consider how the performance of the outsourced service providers affects their business success. It is also often unclear how the type of outsourcing relationship affects business success. Developing a specific outsourcing model is therefore highly useful to the FM industry.

In summary, there are several reasons behind choosing Hong Kong's higher education sector for this study. The sector is one of the most active and sophisticated, best developed and most up-to-date economic sectors. Also, this sector has recently played a highly significant role in Hong Kong. Finally, the local higher education sector has a large economic base with strong competition between universities and institutes. The selected universities and tertiary institutes have similar varieties of FM services, which are offered by different service providers in other institutes. This study thus strongly emphasises FM outsourcing strategies within various contracts, which is one of the variables of the model. Specific FM outsourcing contracts for catering, cleaning, security and maintenance are selected for examination.

CHAPTER TWO

Study goals

This study investigates the performance of outsourcing service providers.

l It aims to establish a clear link between FM performance and business
performance.

l It aims to gain better understanding on the development of outsourcing
relationships between clients and service providers during their contractual periods.

Why this study is needed

l The service providers expect to enhance their own capability in the
formulation of outsourcing strategies.

l The service providers expect to provide better outsourcing services to
their clients by improving their own analytical, managerial, cooperative
and professional skills in solving their relationship management problems.

l The clients expect to gain understanding on how to select the optimum
service providers for their specific FM outsourcing contractual procurement needs.

l The clients expect to maximise value for their money in each FM outsourcing contract through improved effectiveness.

Currently, organisations are required to reduce costs in a competitive environment, and the education institutions in Hong Kong are no exception. They need to have balanced budgets, and they can cut costs by outsourcing. The importance of FM as a means of encouraging learning has been emphasised by the majority of higher-education-related FM studies (Amaratunga and Baldry, 1999; Price et al., 2003; Fianchini, 2006; Lavy, 2008). Vidalakis et al. (2013) also indicate the potential of facilities management and maintenance services to create value, especially for higher education institutions. Such value creation can potentially be greater than that created by the construction of new high-profile facilities. The organisations can improve their revenue by increasing user satisfaction with FM services, thus attracting more students. This study proposes that outsourcing manoeuvres can affect the types and the quality of outsourcing relationships, and thus affect profits.

In summary, clients' satisfaction depends on service providers' services. After understanding the minds of their clients, the service providers can tailor-make their own business strategies for sustainable development. Thus, the purpose of this study is not only to examine the performance of the service providers, but also and more crucially, to understand the standards of service that their

relationships in facilities management, and to predict future FM outsourcing relationships between clients and service providers in the local higher tertiary-education environment.

Insinga and Werle (2000) argue that one of the key concerns behind outsourcing research is to foster the most appropriate form of relationships between a company and service providers. Hätönen and Eriksson (2009) also observe that various economic theories are built on the need to explain the management of inter-organizational relations. Theoretical background behind the different aspects of the outsourcing phenomenon is rather versatile. Accordingly, adopting a singe theoretical view would most probably lead to an oversimplified analysis, especially given the intention to address the five questions of what, why, where, how and when. Hence, it is imperative to understand five theories from the three stages for the theoretical framework in this study. Figure 1 indicates the five selected theories for five key outsourcing questions in this study. This describes a holistic view. Table 1 shows the summary on five theories applying in outsourcing relationships and their functions.

Stage I Stage II Stage III

BIG BANG BAND

WAGON

BARRIERLESS
ORGANIZATIONS ?
RESEARCH
QUESTIONS
WHY?
HOW?
WHAT?
WHERE?
WHEN?
APPLIED
THEORIES
Transaction cost
Resource
View
Organization
based
Relational
(Agency) view
/ (Social Exchange)
Evolution & learning
(Entrepreneurial)
1950 1980 1990 2000 2007

Figure 1 - An overview of the five theories in this study

Theory Definitions Functions
Transaction
Cost
Economics

Organizational effectiveness depends on choosing the appropriate governance structure (internal vs. external), so as to minimize production costs and transaction costs. The level of transaction costs incurred depends on three key transaction attributes—asset specificity, uncertainty, and frequency (Williamson, 1985). Structuring of outsourcing contracts

Agency Cost
Theory

All contracts involve a principal–agent relationship that is characterized by goal incongruence between the principal and the agent. This results in agency costs, specifically, bonding costs (to achieve incentive alignment), monitoring costs (to reduce information asymmetry), and residual loss (due to risk aversion) (Jensen & Meckling, 1976).

Resource
Dependency
Theory

Firms are dependent on their external environment for resources. Resources that the firm cannot generate internally must be acquired through external acquisition. Firms must therefore actively manage the environment and their resource flow, to minimize dependence (Pfeffer & Salancik, 1978).

Addressing
ease of exit

Entrepreneur
ial Actions

Entrepreneurship is an organizational capability that drives economic growth. Entrepreneurial actions, as a process of creative destruction, involve proactive efforts to discover and exploit market opportunities for innovation (Schumpeter, 1936).

Continuous relationship management and information feedback

Social
Exchange
Theory

Interorganizational relationships involve not only legal exchanges between the parties, but also social exchanges based on reciprocity. This requires cooperation and give and take between the parties (Blau, 1964).

Table 1 - Summary on five theories in outsourcing relationships
Facilities management outsourcing services in the higher-education sector
Generally, there are some benefits on application of outsourcing in the higher
education sector (Adegoke and Adegoke, 2013). The growing demand of FM
supporting services at the local universities in past years was accompanied by
advising deployment of outsourcing approach (University Grants Committee,
2010). Although FM outsourcing services at such institutions are increasing,
very little local empirical research has been conducted into the proportion of
outsourcing services in such institutions. As for the kinds of diversified
outsourcing services at the local institutions, there are high risk waste

management, landscaping and horticulture, information technology, capital
project, cleaning, campus security, catering, maintenance for the building
facilities, minor alteration and addition work of premises.

Given that the share of universities' income from tuition fees paid by students
has increased radically over the last 30 years (Carpentier, 2004), the
recruitment of students becomes particularly vital. From a FM perspective,
Vidalakis et al. (2013) investigate the extent to which the quality of facilities
can influence student decision to join a particular higher education institution

because of students' purchase behaviour as an essential determinant of the university marking positioning strategy. Indeed, higher education institutions facilities and learning spaces are, not as important as the course itself but, certainly one of the main aspects that students consider when deciding to join a university (Maringe, 2006; Price et al., 2003). Reynolds and Cain (2006) further discover that a quality built environment is not a sufficient, but necessary condition to recruit and retain students. Given the continuous and increasing pressure on higher education funding, it is imperative to understand the maintenance and procurement on construction of new or refurbishment of existing facilities (Vidalakis et al., 2013).

There are three main reasons for the need to build on this study of FM outsourcing services, particularly in the local higher-education sector. Firstly, outsourcing is one of the procurement approaches used to provide building operation support services in facilities management. Although outsourcing services may not be the best means of solving the typical strategic and operational problems encountered by facilities managers, use of this sourcing strategy in the higher-education sector was scarce but more efficient (Adegoke and Adegoke, 2013). Secondly, very little empirical research has been conducted in this area. Vidalakis et al., (2013) claim that further research is required to reveal the strategic aspects of FM and defines the role of facilities as part of the organisational strategy and culture on improvement of value for money. Thirdly, organisations currently need to adopt outsourcing to take care of built environment in their tertiary institutions because they want to save money (Ferris and Graddy, 1991). Hong Kong's institutions of higher

education are no exception. They too need to balance their budgets, and outsourcing allows them to reduce costs. Universities UK (2009) reports that expenditure on estates and facilities are the second largest cost item after salaries.

Recently, the senior managements of local universities and tertiary institutions have been advised to outsource FM support services in the campuses (University Grants Committee, 2010). Table 2 shows the grants on the University Grants Committee (UGC) - funded institutions for the past ten years. This reflects UGC-funded institutions urgently requiring substantial new and improvement works in the institutions' campuses on recent years. In addition, this also reflects that The Hong Kong Special Area Region Government has a great financial burden on higher education of those UGC-funded institutions. As for the relationship between the quality of

educational
facilities and resultant educational achievement, there is a growing body of
scientific evidence (Duyar, 2010; Fram, 2010; Tanner, 2009). Therefore,
investigation on the effect of facility services on academic achievement is
worthwhile.

Financial Year
2003
/04
2004
/05
2005
/06
2006
/07
2007
/08
2008
/09
2009
/10
2010
/11
2011
/12
2012
/13 1

Grants for UGC-
funded
Institutions 2
($m)

14628 12487 12978 12540 12479 12808 12816 14228 16335
18920

Capital Grants 3 6.2% 5.1% 5.9% 4.4% 4.5% 5.2% 11.6% 14.5% 25.3% 17.8%

Total
Government
Expenditure 2
($m)

243213 242235 233071 226863 234815 312412 289025 301360 364037 380615

Total Amount of
Grants as %
of Total
Government
Expenditure 4

6.0% 5.2% 5.6% 5.5% 5.3% 4.1% 4.4% 4.7% 4.5% 5.0%

Total Amount of
Grants as %
of Total
Government
Expenditure
on Education 4

25.5% 22.9% 23.9% 24.1% 23.2% 17.1% 22.0% 23.4% 24.1% 24.3%

Notes:

1. To tie in with the implementation of the new academic structure, UGC-funded institutions have
admitted two cohorts of students under the old and new academic structures in the 2012/13
academic year.

2. The figures on Grants to UGC-funded Institutions and Total Government Expenditure refer to the
financial year of the Government from April to March.

3. The figures on Capital Grants cover both grants for capital works projects and Alterations, Additions,
Repairs and Improvements (AA&I) projects.

4. The figures on Total Government Expenditure and Total

Government Expenditure on Education are extracted from The Budget.

Source: University Grants Committee of Hong Kong

Table 2 - Statistics on Grants for University Grants Committee-funded Institutions as a whole, 2003-04 to 2012-13

Critical issues for successful outsourcing

Following the publication of a number of seminal studies on facilities management in recent decades, researchers have undertaken many significant explorations of outsourcing. The literature focuses mainly on the reasons for outsourcing, its pros and cons and its critical success factors, and on determining which activities tend to be outsourced in particular industries (Boyson et al., 1999). However, these studies neglect to examine the link between outsourcing arrangements and the performance of service providers.

Coenen et al. (2010) argue that FM corporations should work on managing profitable customer relationships to ensure outsourcing success. Investigation into FM outsourcing relationship types between client and service provider has been initiated on improving service efficiency in specific business.

Although outsourcing has been discussed from many perspectives in different fields, some firms continue to be disadvantaged by the unsatisfactory performance of their outsourcing service providers. As more organisations made the transition to outsourced FM services, the number of reported cases of failure was also increasing (Brown, 2002; Chan, 2008). Baithélemy (2003) address seven common problems for most failed outsourcing efforts. Plane and Green (2012) also explain that the relationships between clients and contractors did not always prosper as anticipated. Hence, there is still possibly a hidden problem on outsourcing failure not yet be observed and solved.

Kavčič and Tavčar (2008) claim that outsourcing can increase an organisation's short-term gains especially in financial terms. However, it may also ruin the company's reputation and success due to poor-quality performance and hidden difficulties. Such problems can exceed the short-term benefits of outsourcing. They also state that trust, based on the mutual long-term interest of both participants, is an important factor determining the success of the relationship between an outsourcing company and an outsourcer. Poor management of the relationship between outsourcers and stakeholders is one possible reason for outsourcing failures; however, no detailed investigations of this topic have recently been undertaken. Moreover, Marshall et al. (2004) report that process studies of outsourcing are rare. It is suggested to use a structured procedure capable of controlling the evolution of a generic outsourcing process (Kakabadse and Kakabadse, 2000). However, there is only limited research on structured partnerships in the field of FM services (Lehtonen and Salonen, 2005). This suggests that our existing knowledge of best-fit FM outsourcing with regard to service providers, clients and users is inadequate and under-developed. It is necessary not only to develop new skills for managing outsourcing relationships, but also to develop the capability to utilise these skills effectively (Harland et al. 2005). The relationship between the company and the service provider should be taken into account when addressing facility-related services (Cigolini et. al., 2011). Plane and Green (2012) also claim that benefits of such relationships in the context of FM procurement, for which partnering and collaboration are essential.

The performance of service providers can affect the quality of FM services, which in turn influences client satisfaction. There is a knowledge gap concerning the link between outsourcing arrangements and service provider performance or client satisfaction (Cigolini, et al., 2011, Jensen, et al. 2012, Lehtonen and Salonen, 2005; Plane, and Green, 2012). The objective of this study is to close this gap. Good relationship management, collaboration and trust-building activities are shown to be just as important as delivering the agreed FM services (Jensen et al., 2012; Kadefors, 2008). The drive towards partnering and collaborative working practices continues to gain pace. For example, the PAS 11000 standard for collaborative business relationship management was introduced as a formal British Standard in December 2010 (British Standards Institute, 2010), and is described in an FM World article as

being 'perfectly logical for the FM sector' (FM World, 2010). Hence, examination of the relationship between outsourcing modes and the performance of FM service providers is needed. Lok et al. (2010) suggest that outsourcing practices can affect outsourcing-relationship types and thus the profit equations of organisations. Clients openly and regularly review their relationships with service providers.

CHAPTER FOUR

Critical analysis of the outsourcing models

Outsourcing activities to a service provider can obviously benefit companies in terms of cost estimation, due to the service provider's familiarity with the work environment and conditions of the installations (Lai, Yik and Jones, 2008). FM outsourcing is an example of the professional mode, with service providers' taking the leading role in professional decision making. However, the poor performance of outsourced service providers cannot be eliminated, and this may pose unforeseen challenges. Scholars continue to debate the question of why so many outsourcing failures are reported if the professional mode constructs the optimal relationship between clients and service providers.

Is it necessary to establish a specific outsourcing-relationship model for facilities management? Before answering this question, it is important to discuss the various possible kinds of outsourcing failures. Baithélemy (2003) claims that one or more of seven problems are responsible for most failed outsourcing efforts, and that firms are generally reluctant to report outsourcing failures. Hätönen and Eriksson (2009) observe that the dynamics and management of outsourcing relationships are very important issues to have become a key managerial interest. The management of the relationships with key suppliers is likely to become increasingly important (Kakabadse and Kakabadse, 2002). The question of how the outsourcing process is carried out is connected to the relationship between the outsourcer and the provider. For example, studying the process in an international context (and thus combining the questions of how and where outsourcing takes place) may shed new light on the outsourcing strategy. Harland et al. (2005) claim that the management of outsourcing relationships, along with the outsourcing process itself, is one of the essential themes of outsourcing research. However, insufficient

attention has been paid to outsourcing failures from the perspective of outsourcing hidden relationships in the entrepreneurial environment (Ikediashi et. al., 2012 and 2013). Establishing a specific outsourcing-relationship model for facilities management may not be the final answer, but it can at least help us to explain and interpret the unseen and complicated scenarios involved.

In short, five outsourcing models are updated in various industries from logistics, different fields, IT, operations management and supply-chain management, but each of which has its own deficiencies. For example, in the field of logistics, prescriptive models of decision making cannot be accurately aligned with outsourcing practice. In the field of IT, the outsourcing relationship management model does not accommodate all of the relationships between vendors and clients at different stages of the framework. The model of four outsourced-outsourcer relationship types does not reflect the evolution of outsourcing relationships.

Consequently, the aim of this research is to apply the most suitable model's rationale to the FM sector. A framework of four outsourcing relationships types (FORT) in the IT industry was proposed (Kishore et al., 2003). This FORT model is used to provide insight into the types of outsourcing relationships exist between clients and service providers. The most interesting trait of this model is that it examines the evolution of companies' outsourcing relationships. Outsourcing relationships are not static; they are liable to change and evolve over time due to changes in the external

environment and
in clients' internal requirements (Kishore et al., 2003). Unlike the FORT model,
other models are not dynamic in nature and do not explore the development
of companies' outsourcing relationships. This study examines the FORT
model in the specific context of the FM industry. This model is suitable and
original because the proposed model covers the relationships between
outsourcing types and outsourcing practices. Further arguments are provided
to support the model of four outsourcing-relationship types. Every outsourcing
model has its own advantages, because of its particular characteristics and
theoretical underpinnings, but also its own disadvantages. Determining which
model is generally best, therefore, is rather a complicated process. Lok and

Finch (2012) state that the FORT model is particularly applicable to the FM
sector on account of the specific advantages. Table 3 indicates the advantages and characteristics of the FORT Framework related to outsourcing relationships in a FM contract.

The FORT Framework
Advantages Characteristics
Like an x-ray machine · Clearly explains and interprets the invisible and complicated
scenarios
· Identifies each stage between the contractual parties
Efficient differentiation
of contracts

· Interpret several kinds of FM contracts simultaneously according to the four relationship types

Easy to handle · Simultaneously check the degree of responsibility and the
strategic effect on the service providers' outsourced portfolio
Effective · Check and update the outsourcing relationships between clients and service providers for each specific FM contract

Versatile · Conveniently applied in different industries
User-friendly · Easy to understand and apply
Flexible · No time constraints on contracts required
Most reliable · Oldest of the five models identified
· Commonly applied in the IT industry
Table 3 - Advantages and characteristics of the FORT Framework

CHAPTER FIVE

The FORT model in facilities management

In the context of the IT industry, the FORT framework is contingent in nature.

Finch (2012) explains that outsourcing relationships have increasingly come to entail processes of mutual support and nurturing. This may include the enhancement of customer relations, improved supplier relationships and the improvement of product or service offerings. Figure 2 indicates the FORT Framework applicable to the FM industry. This new tailor-made proposed FM framework is called Contingency Outsourcing Relationship (CORE) model.

Ownership
and /or
control of
various FM
High
Outsource requiring service
provider's more commitment
(Reliance)

Partner having common goals
(Alliance)

assets
transferred
to service
providers
Low

In-house
(Support)

Outsource enabling acquiring
service provider's technical
expertise
(Alignment)
Low High
Influence of the outsourced FM portfolio on the firm's
competitive positioning and its long-term strategy

Remarks:
(IT dimension): e.g. (Support)
FM dimension: e.g. In-house
Figure 2 - The FORT Framework suitable for FM industry (The CORE
model)
Kishore et al. (2003) explain the mechanism of the FORT model. In the case
of support and alignment relationships, clients make little investment in
service provider specific assets when the level of service-provider involvement
is low. In such cases, client-provider relationships usually operate in the short
term and are fairly specific to outsourced projects and services. Hence, there
is little need for incentives and penalties to be specified in detail. However,
when the level of service-provider involvement is high, clients

make large investments in service provider specific assets. For example, clients become more committed to financing service providers' equipment, technology, systems and skills as part of reliance and alliance connections, which leads to a locked-in relationship. Williamson (1981) describes this phenomenon as 'small numbers opportunism'. Within the alliance relationship, trust is an important mechanism for ensuring that service providers' interests coincide with clients' interests (Sabherwal, 1999).

CHAPTER SIX

Research strategy

In researching the field of management, a researcher needs to adopt many
strategies. Yin (2003) claims that a research strategy should be chosen as a
function of the research situation. This section is to discuss the justification of
selection on appropriate strategies in this study. The relevant key points are
listed as the followings.

1 Importance on selection of suitable research strategy

There are different ways of collecting and analyzing empirical evidence of

the research interest. Research strategy is a way of going about one's
research, embodying a particular style and employing different research
methods (Remenyi et al., 1998). In order to achieve the study aim and
objectives, it is imperative to set optimum research strategy. However,
there are a number of criteria needed in consideration such as scope and
nature of data required for a particular methodology, resource

constraints in terms of time and finance and researcher's personal experience, knowledge and skills (Remenyi et al., 1998; Yin, 2003). In summary, the scope and nature of data of this study are based at the opinions from the service providers and clients. The research study period is very tight and research budget is very limited.

1 Various types of research strategy

There are many strategies including experiment, case study, survey, and ethnography (Remenyi et al., 1998; Saunders et al., 2003; Yin, 2003).
Each strategy has its own specific approach to collect and to analyse empirical data, and each one has its own specific advantages and disadvantages. However, most of these strategies are not suitably applied for the aim and objectives of this research.

i) As for experiments, two main features are manipulation and control but it is inappropriate to set up a laboratory to collect the data in this study. The reason is that experiments fall under the positivist research approach normally used in natural science studies and typically involve two or more experimental groups and a control group. One drawback of experiments is that a laboratory setting is often different from the real world (Collis and Hussey, 2003). The nature of this study is about business management but not natural science.

ii) As for case study, the researcher has `no control over events' and the questions relating to 'why', 'what', or 'how' deal with operational links needing to be traced over time (Yin, 2003). Again, this approach is inappropriate to conduct data collection in this study because the researcher can only focus on a contemporary phenomenon within a real-life context in frequency. In business studies, a common case is a company or parts of a company, but it can also be other things, such as a group of people or event. Some drawbacks of using this strategy include difficulties in finding organisations that are willing to participate in the study; it is difficult to understand the events in a particular period of time. The fact is that it is difficult to identify the suitable local organizations participating in the research as a case study. Moreover, the shortcoming of case studies is described as very time consuming and costly (Collis and Hussey, 2003; Saunders et al., 2003).

iii) Generally speaking, survey is one of the positivist approaches to research. Although this approach has some weaknesses such as low response rate and possible ambiguities in the questions, the benefits such as low cost, convenient access to respondents, mass production, high consistency of research questions, no limitation on time of delivery of questionnaires and completion of questionnaires and fast dispatching of a survey strategy suggested that it was the appropriate methodology in this case. Indeed, surveys are the most popular and commonly used method in business and management research (Remenyi et al., 1998; Saunders et al., 2003).

In this study, the selected number of service providers and staffs in FM department of clients from the local tertiary institutes and universities in the questionnaire surveys are the sample to be taken as a representative of the whole population.

CHAPTER SEVEN

Methodological approach

This study tests whether the Four Outsourcing Relationship Types (FORT) model is applicable to the FM services of Hong Kong's higher education sector through characterising the FM outsourcing relationship types. Ikediashi et al. (2013) consider the importance of outsourcing risks for achieving outsourcing success in the FM sector. In order to holistically build a model for outsourcing FM services, FM strategists should also understand the outsourcing success variables. This study can, in the other way, contribute to existing research on FM by developing another hypothesized model to investigate the hidden relationships between outsourcing success variables and their impact on firm performance in terms of time and strategy. In the following sections, there is an analysis of outsourcing relationship from these theoretical perspectives to develop corollaries about the relationships between

the strategic manoeuvres identified and the different dimensions of outsourcing relationship. There are nine corollaries in this research. Table 4
summarizes the theories discussed, the key concepts used, and the resulting
corollaries developed.

Theory /
Concept

Key concepts / Strategic
Manoeuvres

Corollaries

Four FM
outsourcing
dimensions

FM strategists and types of FM
outsourcing contract → FM
outsourcing dimensions

(Clients and Service providers) C1a, C1b: Clients' and Service providers' evaluations regarding four
outsourcing relationship dimensions rendered to them are not different according to the background of
construction professionals and types of current outsourcing contracts.

Transaction Cost
Economics

Reduced asset specificity by
minimizing customization →
outsourcing relationship

(Clients and Service providers) C2a, C2b: Clients' and Service providers' evaluations regarding
minimizing customization rendered to them are not different according to the background of construction
professionals and types of current outsourcing contracts.

Agency Cost
Theory

Reduced monitoring cost by
enhancing process maturity →
outsourcing relationship
Mitigation of residual loss by retaining
in-house competence → outsourcing
relationship

(Clients & Service providers) C3a, C3b: Clients' and Service providers' evaluations regarding enhancing
process maturity rendered to them are not different according to the background of construction
professionals and types of current outsourcing contracts.
(Clients and Service providers) C4a, C4b: Clients' and Service providers' evaluations regarding retaining
in-house competence rendered to them are not different according to the background of construction
professionals and types of current outsourcing contracts.

Resource
Dependency
Theory

Diluting supplier concentration
through multiple sourcing →
outsourcing relationship
Reduced switching costs through
vendor interoperability
→ outsourcing relationship

(Clients and Service providers) C5a, C5b: Clients' and Service providers' evaluations regarding multiple
sourcing rendered to them are not different according to the background of construction professionals
and types of current outsourcing contracts.
(Clients and Service providers) C6a, C6b: Clients' and Service providers' evaluations regarding
leveraging on vendor interoperability rendered to them are not different according to the background of
construction professionals and types of current outsourcing

contracts.

Entrepreneurial
Actions

Enhanced entrepreneurial capability
through proactive sensing →
outsourcing relationship

(Clients and Service providers) C7a, C7b: Clients' and Service providers' evaluations regarding proactive
sensing rendered to them are not different according to the background of construction professionals and
types of current outsourcing contracts.

Social Exchange
Theory

Building relational reciprocity
through enhanced partnership
quality → outsourcing relationship

(Clients and Service providers) C8a, C8b: Clients' and Service providers' evaluations regarding
enhancing partnership quality rendered to them are not different according to the background of
construction professionals and types of current outsourcing contracts.

The FORT
model

Outsourcing relationship dimensions
→ outsourcing relationship types

(Clients and Service providers) C9: Outsourcing relationship dimensions (Ownership, Control,
Competitive Position and Long Term Plan) is related to outsourcing relationship types and the strength of
the relationships is moderated by those outsourcing types.

Table 4 - Summary of corollaries on outsourcing relationship

Strategic manoeuvres for outsourcing relationship: a conceptual framework

There are two parts composing the research model in this study. This first part is about outsourcing relationships and the second part is about outsourcing category. With the combination of two parts, a research model was developed for this study. It firstly sets out the relationships between the independent variable (outsourcing relationship manoeuvres) and dependent variable (four outsourcing relationship dimensions). It secondly sets out the relationships between the independent variable (four outsourcing relationship dimensions) and dependent variable (outsourcing category). The interaction and combined effect of these independent variables will determine the value of the dependent variables for the two parts.

In the first part of the model, the factors perceived to be of principal relevance were discussed. Outsourcing relationships include two parts: extent of substitution and strategic importance or impact. The four relationship dimensions can be measured objectively and subjectively and they are inter-related and intra-related. These factors can form the dependent variables of this part. Outsourcing relationship manoeuvres are supported by five identified theories. These factors form the independent variables of this part. In the second part of the model, the factors perceived to be of principal relevance were discussed. Outsourcing category of a project includes in-house, service provider with commitment, service provider with technical expertise and partner. The factors can be measured objectively and subjectively and they are inter-related and intra-related. These factors can form the dependent variables of this part. Again, outsourcing relationships include two parts: extent of substitution and strategic importance or impact. The four relationship dimensions can be measured objectively and subjectively and they are inter-related and intra-related. These factors form the independent variables of this part. Figure 3 provides a graphic representation of the strategic manoeuvres and the theoretical perspectives from which they are derived.

Corollary 1 (Relationships between four outsourcing relationships measured by critical success factors for outsourcing strategies and two FM stakeholders)

Corollary 2 – Corollary 8 (Relationships between five outsourcing manoeuvres and two FM stakeholders)

Corollary 9 (Relationships between four outsourcing relationships measured by critical success factors for outsourcing strategies and four FM outsourcing categories)

C9

C7 C8 C5 & C6

Four Outsourcing

Relationship Dimensions

Extent of substitution: Ownership & Control

Strategic impact: Competitive position &

Long term plan
Outsourcing Categories
Inhouse (Support), SP with technical expertise
(Alignment), SP with commitment (Reliance) &
Partner (Alliance)
Transaction
Cost
Economics
Minimizing
customization
(asset
specificity)
Enhancing process
maturity
(information asymmetry)
Retaining in-house
competence
(residual loss)
Proactive sensing
(entrepreneurial capability)
Enhanced partnership
quality
Social Exchange Theory Entrepreneurial Actions
Agency Cost Theory
C2
C3 & 4
Background
C1

Figure 3: Research model on contingency model for outsourcing relationships in FM sector

CHAPTER EIGHT

Testing the nine proposed corollaries

The main objective of this section is to test the nine corollaries concerning the determinants of outsourcing relationship dimensions, strategic manoeuvres, clients' and service providers' evaluation regarding outsourcing category and outsourcing relationship types. The statistical techniques employed for testing these corollaries 1 to 8 are the Mann-Whitney U test (only two groups of continuous variables in the background of construction professionals) and Kruskal-Wallis test (continuous variable for three or more groups in the types of current outsourcing contracts) and corollary 9 is Multi-nominal Logistic Regression (similar to logistic regression, but more general as the dependent variable not restricted to two categories in four outsourcing categories). Nine main corollaries have been tested as follows.

Testing the corollary 1

As seen earlier, researchers and practitioners have found that IT clients consider four dimensions in their assessments of outsourcing category between clients and service providers (Kishore et. al., 2003).

* Support: requiring assistance
* Alignment: technical expertise
* Reliance: service commitment
* Alliance: common goals

Client and Service Provider - C1 (a)

The Mann-Whitney test has been used to test for differences between two independent groups on a continuous measure. There is no statistical significant difference with a two-tailed p value. The probability value (p) is not less than or equal to 0.05, that to say there is no statistically significant difference in the perceived four outsourcing relationship dimensions rendered to two kinds of FM strategists.

Performance of
Outsourcing Services
Evaluation of outsourcing categories on
current & future FM contracts of clients and
service providers

Characteristics of
FM strategists in
clients & Service
Providers (SP)

Resource Dependency
Theory
Multiple sourcing
(supplier concentration)
Leveraging vendor

interoperability
(switching costs)

Result on Nonparametric Tests (Clients and Service providers - C1a): Mann-Whitney U Test comparing four FM outsourcing relationship dimensions in FM professions of building and building services

Client and Service Provider - C1 (b)

To test the validity of this hypothesis, the Kruskal-Wallis test was used to examine the differences of FM strategists' evaluation of the four outsourcing relationship dimensions rendered to them in different types of current outsourcing contracts. There is no statistical significant difference with a p value. The probability value (p) is not less than or equal to 0.05. There are no significant statistical differences in FM strategists' evaluation of the four outsourcing relationship dimensions rendered to them in different types of current outsourcing contracts. This means that all types of profession render the same perceived four outsourcing relationship dimensions from the FM strategists' point of view, in terms of the outsourcing contracts.

Result on Nonparametric Tests (Clients and Service providers - C1b): Kruskal-Wallis Test comparing four FM outsourcing relationship dimensions in four FM Outsourcing contracts (Building maintenance, Security, Cleaning and Catering)

Testing corollaries 2 to 8
Clients and Service Providers (C2a – C8a)
The Mann-Whitney test has been used to test for differences of the perceived
strategic manoeuvres (Five theories) rendered to two kinds of FM strategists.

Result on Nonparametric Tests (Clients and Service providers): Mann-Whitney
U Test comparing strategic manoeuvres (Five theories) in FM professions of
building and building services

Clients and Service Providers (C2b – C8b)
To test the validity of this hypothesis, the Kruskal-Wallis test was used to
examine the differences of FM strategists' evaluation of the strategic

manoeuvres (Five theories) rendered to them in different types of current
outsourcing contracts.

Result on Nonparametric Tests (Clients and Service providers): Kruskal-Wallis
Test comparing strategic manoeuvres (Five theories) in four FM Outsourcing
contracts (Building maintenance, Security, Cleaning and Catering)

Testing corollary 9
Dependent variable: A categorical variable that record whether the strategist
was satisfactory. The value of mulit-Nominal logistic regression may be high
(Likert Scale 4 or 5) or low (Likert Scale 1 or 2). For example, the value "1"
indicates the high degree of satisfaction of the specific outsourcing category,
while the value "0" indicates the low degree of satisfaction of the

specific
outsourcing category on contingent approaches of the specific FM outsourcing
contract. In this research, the multi-nominal logistic regression is used to
analyse the categories of FM outsourcing relationship types from clients and
service providers. This test is used to observe and predict the relationships.
Table 5 shows the data analysis of Multi-Nominal Logistic Regression.

Types of
Variable
Variables
(Client)
Variables
(Service
Provider)
Definition
Factors Y1 – Y4 Y1 – Y4 Types of FM Contract
Y1: Building maintenance
Y2: Security
Y3: Cleaning
Y4: Catering
Dependent OC1 – OC4 OC1 – OC4 FM Outsourcing Categories
In-house team, Commitment,
Technical expertise, Common goals
Independent SO1 – SO5 SO1 – SO5
FM Outsourcing Dimensions
Ownership of FM assets
Independent SC1 – SC8 SC1 – SC3 Control of FM assets
Independent CP1 – CP6 CP1 – CP17 Influence on competitive position
Independent LP1 – LP8 LP1 – LP11 Influence on long term plan
Table 5 - Factors, dependent variables and independent variables in

Multi-Nominal Logistic Regression

24

Category of outsourcing relationship of a specific kind of outsourcing contract

between client and service provider

Client

To predict the category of the outsourcing relationships, the Mulit-Nominal

Logistic Regression was used to determine the different types of current

crucial outsourcing contracts between the clients and service providers from

the perspective of clients. The types of outsourcing category on clients' point

of views will be investigated by applying the FM outsourcing relationship

dimensions in four FM outsourcing contracts through mulit-Nominal Logistic

Regression. Table 6 indicates the details of data from this Regression. There

are total 188 valid cases and 14 missing cases from the clients' respondents.

According to the case processing summary, the model category is Technical

Expertise, with 33.5% of the cases. Thus, the null model classifies correctly

33.5% of the time. This classification table shows the practical results of using

the multinomial logistic regression model.

Number

of case

Marginal

Percentage

Types of outsourcing category Inhouse 46 24.5%

Service commitment 41 21.8%

Technical expertise 63 33.5%
Common goals 38 20.2%

Measurement of Ownership of various FM assets transferred by you

low 80 42.6%
high 108 57.4%

Measurement of Control of various FM assets transferred by you

low 56 29.8%
high 132 70.2%

Measurement of influence of the outsourced FM portfolio on our competitive position

low 75 39.9%
high 113 60.1%

Measurement of influence of the outsourced FM portfolio on our long-term plan

low 62 33.0%
high 126 67.0%
Valid 188 100.0%
Missing 14
Total 202
Subpopulation 25 a

a. The dependent variable has only one value observed in 2 (8.0%) subpopulations.

Table 6 - Case Processing Summary (Clients)

Table 7 indicates the observed and predicted frequencies on category of FM

outsourcing relationship types from clients. On prediction of the type of future
building maintenance, security, cleaning and catering contracts, there is an
inclination to the types of inhouse and technical expertise. In

summary,
degree of importance on the types of inhouse and technical expertise
outsourcing categories is the highest to the four FM outsourcing contracts.

(a) (b) (c) (d) (e) Types of outsourcing
category
Frequency Percentage
(f) (g) Pearson
Residual
(f) (g)
Building
maintenance
low low low low Inhouse 3 3.100 -.065 21.4% 22.1%
low low high high Service commitment 0 .035 -.189 .0% 1.8%
high high high low Technical expertise 1 .908 .110 25.0% 22.7%
high high high high Common goals 6 5.374 .291 15.8% 14.1%
Security low low low low Inhouse 3 3.082 -.053 21.4% 22.0%
low low high high Service commitment 0 .030 -.175 .0% 1.5%
high high high low Technical expertise 1 .977 .027 25.0% 24.4%
high high high high Common goals 3 3.979 -.531 11.1% 14.7%
Cleaning low low low low Inhouse 3 2.401 .437 27.3% 21.8%
low low high high Service commitment 0 .026 -.163 .0% 1.3%
high high high low Technical expertise 1 1.567 -.527 16.7% 26.1%
high high high high Common goals 3 3.668 -.379 12.5% 15.3%
Catering low low low low Inhouse 2 1.295 .699 33.3% 21.6%
low low high high Service commitment 0 .022 -.151 .0% 1.1%
high high high low Technical expertise 2 2.224 -.177 25.0% 27.8%
high high high high Common goals 0 .158 -.433 .0% 15.8%

The percentages are based on total observed frequencies in each subpopulation.

Remarks: a) Major types of FM outsourcing contract in the questionnaire survey; b) Influence
of the outsourced FM portfolio on our long-term plan; c) Influence of the outsourced FM

portfolio on our competitive position; d) Control of various FM assets transferred by you; e)
Ownership of various FM assets transferred by you; f) Observed and g) Predicted
Table 7 - Observed and Predicted Frequencies on category of FM outsourcing relationship types from clients
Service Provider
To predict the category of the outsourcing relationships, the Mulit-Nominal
Logistic Regression was used to determine the different types of current
crucial outsourcing contracts between the clients and service providers from
the perspective of service provider. The types of outsourcing category on
service provider's point of views will be investigated by applying the FM
outsourcing relationship dimensions in four FM outsourcing contracts through
mulit-Nominal Logistic Regression. Table 8 indicates the details of data from
this Regression. There are total 160 valid cases and 3 missing cases from the
service providers' respondents. According to the case processing summary,
the model category is Inhouse, with 29.4% of the cases. Thus, the null model

classifies correctly 29.4% of the time. This classification table shows the
practical results of using the multinomial logistic regression model. Number
of case
Marginal
Percentage

Types of outsourcing category Inhouse 47 29.4%
Service commitment 41 25.6%
Technical expertise 40 25.0%
Common goals 32 20.0%

Measurement of Ownership of various FM assets transferred by you

low 10 6.3%
high 150 93.8%

Measurement of Control of various FM assets transferred by you

low 16 10.0%
high 144 90.0%

Measurement of Influence of the outsourced FM portfolio on our competitive position

low 10 6.3%
high 150 93.8%

Measurement of Influence of the outsourced FM portfolio on our long-term plan

low 10 6.3%
high 150 93.8%
Valid 160 100.0%
Missing 3
Total 163
Subpopulation 10 a

a. The dependent variable has only one value observed in 1 (10.0%) subpopulations.

Table 8 - Case Processing Summary (Service provider)

If the significance value is small (less than 0.05), then the model does not
adequately fit the data. In this case, table 9 indicates its value greater than
0.1, so the data are consistent with the model assumptions. The Pearson

residual is a measure of the difference between the observed and predicted
values. Large Pearson residuals can indicate covariate patterns that are not
well fit by the model. In classification and validation, cross tabulating observed
response categories with predicted categories helps to determine how well the
model identifies clients' and service providers' preferences.

Chi-Square df Sig.
Clients Pearson 17.803 57 1.000
Deviance 19.588 57 1.000
Service
providers
Pearson 3.902 18 1.000
Deviance 4.659 18 .999

Table 9 - Goodness-of-Fit (Clients and Service providers)

Table 10 indicates the observed and predicted frequencies on category of FM
outsourcing relationship types from service providers. On prediction of the
future building maintenance, security, cleaning and catering contracts, there is
an equally inclination to the type of inhouse outsourcing category. In summary,
degree of importance on the types of inhouse and common goals outsourcing
categories is the highest to the four FM outsourcing contracts.

(a) (b) (c) (d) (e) Types of
outsourcing
category
Frequency Percentage
(f) (g) Pearson
Residual
(f) (g)

Building
maintenance
low low low low Inhouse 2 1.999 .001 50.0% 50.0%
high high high high Common goals 12 11.066 .311 20.0% 18.4%
Security low low low low Inhouse 1 1.000 .000 50.0% 50.0%
high high high low Technical
expertise
1 .833 .200 20.0% 16.7%
high high high high Common goals 6 6.552 -.239 17.1% 18.7%
Cleaning low low low low Inhouse 1 1.000 -.001 50.0% 50.0%
high high high high Common goals 4 4.370 -.197 17.4% 19.0%
Catering low low low low Inhouse 1 1.001 -.001 50.0% 50.0%
high high high high Common goals 5 5.012 -.006 19.2% 19.3%

The percentages are based on total observed frequencies in each subpopulation.

Remarks: a) Major types of FM outsourcing contract in the questionnaire survey;b) Influence of the outsourced FM portfolio on our long-term plan; c) Influence of the outsourced FM portfolio on our competitive position;d) Control of various FM assets transferred by you; e) Ownership of various FM assets transferred by you; f) Observed and g) Predicted

Table 10 - Observed and Predicted Frequencies on category of FM outsourcing relationship types from service providers

CHAPTER NINE

Findings

The local Government funded vocational training institutes and seven universities in this study represent more than 90% of the FM industry in Hong Kong's higher educational sectors. The total number in the study sample was 38 FM respondents from clients and 34 FM respondents from service providers who participated in this study. The main outputs of frequency analysis reveal that the study sample was biased towards the master degree holders, where the percentage of those FM professionals (clients and service providers) was very high being 74% and 64% respectively, and the study sample was well educated. With regard to the FM working experience of the respondents, it has been indicated that almost 60% of the clients' respondents

had equal or more than three years; the percentage of service providers' respondents who had equal or more than three years was 80%.

Results of testing corollaries 1 – 8 (clients)

Table 11 summarises the results of analysis on the types of outsourcing
category on the FM relationship from clients. According to the evaluations of
clients' construction professionals on the ownership of various FM assets
transferred, infrastructure technology, computing system and communication
system rendered to them are same, but professional knowledge and efficiency
of equipment rendered to them are different. As for the types of current
outsourcing contracts on the same dimension, professional knowledge,
infrastructure technology, computing system, communication system and
efficiency of equipment rendered to the clients are same.

Corollaries (1 – 8) Results

Ownership of various FM assets transferred

C1a: Clients' evaluations regarding ownership (professional knowledge
and efficiency of equipment) rendered to them are not different
according to the background of construction professionals.

Rejected

C1a: Clients' evaluations regarding ownership (infrastructure technology,
computing system and communication system) rendered to them are not
different according to the background of construction professionals.

Accepted

C1b: Clients' evaluations regarding ownership (professional knowledge,
infrastructure technology, computing system, communication

system and
efficiency of equipment) rendered to them are not different according to
the types of current outsourcing contracts.

Accepted

Control of various FM assets transferred

C1a: Clients' evaluations regarding control (infrastructure and equipment) rendered to them are not different according to the background of construction professionals.

Rejected

C1a: Clients' evaluations regarding control (human resources, daily
routine operation, job, deadlines, co-ordination meetings and expense)
rendered to them are not different according to the background of construction professionals.

Accepted

C1b: Clients' evaluations regarding control (infrastructure, equipment,
human resources, daily routine operation, job, deadlines, co-ordination
meetings and expense) rendered to them are not different according to
the types of current outsourcing contracts.

Accepted

Influence of the outsourced FM portfolio on competitive position

C1a and C1b: Clients' evaluations regarding competitive position (competence, accuracy, productivity, technical competence, comprehensive service and time frame) rendered to them are not different according to the background of construction professionals and
types of current outsourcing contracts.

Accepted

Influence of the outsourced FM portfolio on our long-term plan C1a: Clients' evaluations regarding long-term plan (policy and plan) Rejected

rendered to them are not different according to the background of construction professionals.

C1a: Clients' evaluations regarding long-term plan (work, safety and health, human resources, administration, quality and environmental protection) rendered to them are not different according to the background of construction professionals.

Accepted

C1b: Clients' evaluations regarding long-term plan (policy, plan, work, safety and health, human resources, administration, quality and environmental protection) rendered to them are not different according to the types of current outsourcing contracts.

Accepted

C2a and C2b: Clients' evaluations regarding minimizing process customization rendered to them are not different according to the background of construction professionals and types of current outsourcing contracts.

Accepted

C3a and C3b: Clients' evaluations regarding enhancing process maturity rendered to them are not different according to the background of construction professionals and types of current outsourcing contracts.

Accepted

C4a and C4b: Clients' evaluations regarding retaining in-house competence rendered to them are not different according to the background of construction professionals and types of current outsourcing contracts.

Accepted

C5a and C5b: Clients' evaluations regarding multiple sourcing rendered to them are not different according to the background of construction professionals and types of current outsourcing contracts.

Accepted

C6a and C6b: Clients' evaluations regarding leveraging on vendor interoperability rendered to them are not different according to the background of construction professionals and types of current outsourcing contracts.

Accepted

C7a and C7b: Clients' evaluations regarding proactive sensing rendered to them are not different according to the background of construction professionals and types of current outsourcing contracts.

Accepted

C8a and C8b: Clients' evaluations regarding enhancing partnership quality rendered to them are not different according to the background of construction professionals and types of current outsourcing contracts.

Accepted

Table 11 - Analysis on the types of outsourcing category on the FM relationship by clients

According to the evaluations of clients' construction professionals on the control of various FM assets transferred, human resources, daily routine operation, job, deadlines, co-ordination meetings and expense are same, but

infrastructure and equipment rendered to them are different. As for the types
of current outsourcing contracts on the same dimension, infrastructure,
equipment, human resources, daily routine operation, job, deadlines, co-
ordination meetings and expense rendered to the clients are same.

According to the evaluations of clients' construction professionals and types of
current outsourcing contracts on the influence of the outsourced FM portfolio

on competitive position, competence, accuracy, productivity, technical
competence, comprehensive service and time frame rendered to the clients
are same.

According to the evaluations of clients' construction professionals on the
influence of the outsourced FM portfolio on our long-term plan, policy and plan
rendered to them are different. As for the evaluations of clients' construction
professionals and types of current outsourcing contracts on the same
dimension, policy, plan, work, safety and health, human resources,
administration, quality and environmental protection, minimizing process
customization, enhancing process maturity, retaining in-house competence,
multiple sourcing, leveraging on vendor interoperability, proactive sensing,
enhancing partnership quality rendered to the clients are same.

Results of testing corollaries 1 – 8 (service providers)

Table 12 summarises the results of analysis on the types of

outsourcing
category on the FM relationship from service providers. According to the
evaluations of service providers' construction professionals and the types of
current outsourcing contracts on the ownership of various FM assets
transferred, equipment or machinery, professional knowledge, completion on
request, capability, resources, rendered to them are same.

Corollaries (1 – 8) Results

Ownership of various FM assets transferred

C1a and C1b: Service providers' evaluations regarding ownership (equipment or machinery, professional knowledge, completion on request,
capability and resources) rendered to them are not different according to
the background of construction professionals and types of current outsourcing contracts.

Accepted

Control of various FM assets transferred

C1a and C1b: Service providers' evaluations regarding control (professional knowledge, finishing on time and co-ordination meetings)
rendered to them are not different according to the background of construction professionals and types of current outsourcing contracts.

Accepted

Influence of the outsourced FM portfolio on competitive position

C1a and C1b: Service providers' evaluations regarding competitive position (financial capability, human resources, assistance, capability,
accuracy, productivity, technical competence, focus, responsibility, conduct, courteousness, understanding, comprehensive service,

responsibilities, quality, satisfaction and expectation) rendered to them are

Accepted

not different according to the background of construction professionals
and types of current outsourcing contracts.
Influence of the outsourced FM portfolio on our long-term plan
C1a and C1b: Service providers' evaluations regarding long-term plan
(competing job, policy, plan, work, safety and health, human resources,
administration, quality, social responsibility, value-added services and
environmental protection) rendered to them are not different according to
the background of construction professionals and types of current outsourcing contracts.

Accepted

C2a and C2b: Service providers' evaluations regarding minimizing process
customization rendered to them are not different according to the
background of construction professionals and types of current outsourcing
contracts.

Accepted

C3a and C3b: Service providers' evaluations regarding enhancing process
maturity rendered to them are not different according to the background of
construction professionals and types of current outsourcing contracts.

Accepted

C4a and C4b: Service providers' evaluations regarding retaining in-house

competence rendered to them are not different according to the background of construction professionals and types of current outsourcing
contracts.

Accepted

C5a and C5b: Service providers' evaluations regarding multiple sourcing
rendered to them are not different according to the background of construction professionals and types of current outsourcing contracts.

Accepted

C6a and C6b: Service providers' evaluations regarding leveraging on
vendor interoperability rendered to them are not different according to the
background of construction professionals and types of current outsourcing
contracts.

Accepted

C7a and C7b: Service providers' evaluations regarding proactive sensing
rendered to them are not different according to the background of construction professionals and types of current outsourcing contracts.

Accepted

C8a and C8b: Service providers' evaluations regarding enhancing
partnership quality rendered to them are not different according to the
background of construction professionals and types of current outsourcing
contracts.

Accepted

Table 12 - Analysis on the types of outsourcing category on the FM

relationship by service providers
According to the evaluations of service providers' construction professionals
and the types of current outsourcing contracts on the control of various FM
assets transferred, professional knowledge, finishing on time and co-
ordination meetings rendered to them are same. According to the evaluations
of service providers' construction professionals and the types of current
outsourcing contracts on the influence of the outsourced FM portfolio on
competitive position, financial capability, human resources, assistance,
capability, accuracy, productivity, technical competence, focus, responsibility,
conduct, courteousness, understanding, comprehensive service,
responsibilities, quality, satisfaction and expectation rendered to them are
same.

According to the evaluations of service providers' construction professionals
and the types of current outsourcing contracts on the influence of the
outsourced FM portfolio on our long-term plan, competing job, policy, plan,
work, safety and health, human resources, administration, quality, social
responsibility, value-added services, environmental protection, minimizing
process customization, enhancing process maturity, retaining in-house
competence, multiple sourcing, leveraging on vendor interoperability,

proactive sensing and enhancing partnership quality rendered to them are same.

Analysis on matching the results of clients and service providers, Corollary 9

A key to analysis is to identify which types of outsourcing relationships have impact on the standard and quality of the outsourcing services in the major FM outsourcing contracts such as building maintenance, security, cleaning and catering in the Hong Kong's higher education industry. From the result, the clients can obtain an understanding of their predicted percentage of the FM outsourcing relationship type for the specific type of FM contract. The service provider can also evaluate the 'future' possible performance in the specific outsourcing contract.

The Pearson residual is a measure of the difference between the observed and predicted values. Small Pearson residuals can indicate covariate patterns that are well fit by the model. The types of outsourcing category for the specific types of FM contract are based by two variables which are the optimum predicted percentage and the small Pearson residuals. Table 13 indicates the outsourcing relationship type with the predicted highest degree of importance of the specific critical FM outsourcing contract from clients and service providers. Predicted good FM outsourcing performance on

the specific
outsourcing contract is achieved by matching the predicted type of outsourcing category from client and relevant service provider. In summary,
degree of importance on the type of inhouse outsourcing category is the
highest to the future building maintenance, security, cleaning and catering

contracts. On further prediction of these four FM outsourcing contracts, there
is also an inclination to the type of technical expertise outsourcing category
from clients but to the type of common goals outsourcing category from
service provider.

(a) (b) (c) (d) (e) Types of
outsourcing
category

Clients
Percentage

Service
Provider
Percentage
(f) (g) (f) (g)

Building
maintenance

Low low low low Inhouse 21.4% 22.1% 50.0% 50.0%
High high high low Technical

expertise 25.0% 22.7% - -
high high high high Common goals - - 20.0% 18.4%

Security

low low low low Inhouse 21.4% 22.0% 50.0% 50.0%
high high high low Technical

expertise 25.0% 24.4% - -
high high high high Common goals - - 17.1% 18.7%
Cleaning
low low low low Inhouse 27.3% 21.8% 50.0% 50.0%
high high high low Technical
expertise 16.7% 26.1% - -
high high high high Common goals - - 17.4% 19.0%
Catering
low low low low Inhouse 33.3% 21.6% 50.0% 50.0%
high high high low Technical
expertise 25.0% 27.8% - -
high high high high Common goals - - 19.2% 19.3%

Remarks: a) Major types of FM outsourcing contract in the questionnaire survey; b) Influence of the outsourced FM portfolio on long-term plan; c) Influence of the outsourced FM portfolio on competitive position; d) Control of various FM assets transferred; e) Ownership of various FM assets transferred; f) Observed and g) Predicted

Table 13 - Predicted FM outsourcing relationship types of the FM outsourcing contracts survey in the current Hong Kong's higher education sector

Chapter 10 - Discussion and Conclusion

Understanding on FM outsourcing relationships in Higher Education Sector

The analysis of the simultaneous relationships between FM outsourcing relationship types and dimensions (substitution of ownership, substitution of control, competitive position and long-term planning) enhances the overall understanding of FM outsourcing relationships. The empirical investigation reveals a significant relationship between FM outsourcing relationship types and services in the context of Hong Kong's higher education sector. Clients and service providers have indicated that applying the FM outsourcing relationship types improves the quality of the services. Meanwhile, the results of the hypotheses testing indicate that FM outsourcing relationship types are used in related services; that is, the outsourcing categories of a specific FM outsourcing contract will be achieved through prediction at the level of substitution of ownership, substitution of control, competitive positions and long-term planning.

Importantly, this research establishes a link between 'high quality FM outsourcing service' and potential increases in substitution of ownership, substitution of control, competitive positions and long-term planning. The relationship between FM outsourcing relationship types and service is statistically significant. The majority of previous FM outsourcing studies has discussed the causes of service providers' substandard outsourcing performance without considering the relationships among the four FM outsourcing relationship dimensions in FM outsourcing contracts. This research investigates these relationships from both the clients and the service providers' perspectives, with regard to FM outsourcing relationship

categories
and services.

CHAPTER TEN

Future research directions

Although the focus of this study is the importance of FM outsourcing relationship types and dimensions in Hong Kong's higher education sector, and their centrality has been confirmed, the researcher believes that the demand and supply of FM services will play a major role in the future of the higher education industry. As previously noted, universities' financial costs have recently increased, which means that the FM client-strategists must plan updated FM strategies to solve the current and future financial problems. As a result, further research is required to explore the relationships among critical FM outsourcing contracts.

Finally, it is not possible for any single study to cover every aspect of a topic, and this study is no exception. The 'evolution and revolution' of FM outsourcing relationship types and dimensions will continue, and thus the topic deserves further investigation. For instance, it is important to investigate how clients and service providers can manage the financial aspects of FM outsourcing contracts to efficiently improve overall FM outsourcing performance services. These concepts might also be applied to other advanced building assets in other business sectors, such as contemporary office buildings, airports, hotels and hospitals.

Limitations of the FORT model

However, the concept of the evolution of the outsourcing relationships types has its limitation if companies and public bodies have their own subsidiary property management firms or hire service providers for fixed client-service provider relationships at the outset. It is also possible that the pace of FM practices nationally differ between western and eastern countries. FM is a relatively new and fast developing profession in the service industry (Hui, et al., 2013). The new concept of evolution of outsourcing relationships between the FM stakeholders is relatively innovative to the local FM professionals in the Asian Pacific regions.

Outsourcing FM Service Brings Advantages To Offices

Why do some organizations need to implement outsourcing strategy? If the organization does not implement outsourcing strategy, what disadvantages to the organization ? The fundamental elements of outsourcing, it is necessary to have a picture that incorporates all of the elements include its nature, services, strategies management of relationships and particularly its theoretical models.

Firstly, we need to understand why the organization ought choose to implement outsourcing strategy. We need to know that service providers need to implement effective strategy in order to let its employees can feel comfortable to work in the organization's office, e.g. facility management outsourcing service, property management, office clearning, maintenance , securty and catering services.

All of these services are elements to any organizational environment. Hence, if the organizatios can attempt to implement outsourcing strategy for above element services. Consequently, it is possible to help this organization to reduce much extra expenditure to compare it chooses to set up cleaning department, security department, property management , facility managment departments, catering department to deal itself daily element services for itself employees working environment in its office building.Hence, it seems that any one of these any one element office service ought be implemeted outsoucing service from outsourcing service provider.

Why outsourcing service may help this organization to reduce cost expenditure to compare it implements to set up different departments ? The main benefit to this organization, it must not need to employ many employees, e.g. cleaning, catering, property and facility management, security employees hen it decides to outsource these services from outsourcing service providers. Hence, it must reduce to spend salaries expenditure when it decides to outsource service providers to help it to do these any one office services for its office benefits.

In fact, outsourcing service may be improved service performance, e.g. cleaning , security, catering, Fm, property management service performance, due to this outsourcing service provider hopes this organization can continue choose its services for long term among of many same service providers in the outsoucring office service competitive market. Otherwise, if it only employs cleaning, security, catering, FM , property management service employees. They may leave this organization when they feel low salaries, or change their career, change another new employer. Otherwise, when this organization chooses outsourcing services to outsoucring service providers, it won't need to worry about these employees.

Outsoucring is clearly quite common in many companies around the world. Outsouring from " out"and " service". which together " describe an external source is a management approach that delegates to an external agent the operational responsibility for processes or services previously delivered by the enterprise itself. It can be defined as the purchase of a product or a service that was previously provided internally" (Bailhelemy , 2003 (p.92), eLMUTI & Kathawala, 2000 (p,114), Lankford and Parsa, 1999 (p,312).

However, there is much debate in the managment, literature regardly the definition of outsourcing (Gilley & Rasheed, 2000). resolve this confusion by providing a broad finition for outsourcing that includes the following arrangements and concepts: internal vs external sourcing (Scheuing, 1989); Strategic make -or - outsourcing decisions (Virolarinen, 1998) and make- or-buy and focus decisions) Knight & Hurland, 2000).

In fact, in transaction cost economic theory, it can explain why outsourcing office service which can earn more benefit to compare employing service employees. The reason is indicated Williamson (1985) considers the relative advantages of handling transactions through internal (hierarchy) or external (market) organizational forms. Outsourcing offers an organizational solution what can reduce production costs by leveraging on market economies, though this must be balanced against associated transactions costs.

So, the author explains that why organizations ought need to outsource service during this stage, companies outsourced noncore business processes basically to cut operational costs. Outsoucing which was a tool to make organizations more efficient economic units for profit maximization mainly occurred domestically.

He believed that the relationship were managed in an arms-length manner, relying on contracts. Moreover, the level of transaction costs incurred depends on characteristics of the outsourced activities, in particular, asset specificity, uncertainty and transaction frequency,

However, typical commercial buildings, every organization 's office must need to implement saving of costing strategy for improving competitive edges and outcomes some functions, for example maintenance works critiically consideration on performance in terms of technical knowledge, skill, equipment, speed, flexible manpower to outsourcing service providers as well as outsourcing service providers can manage more effective and efficient building maintenance serving jobs for the office owner, such as air-conditioning, mechanical ventilation, fire services, life/escalators, plumbing/drainage, lighting , laundry and catering installations, even simple service jobs, such as cleaning and security deliver higher level of quality services to compare the organization (office owner) employs these service employees for itself office services.

On conclusion, it seems that any middle and large size organizations ought choose to give outsourcing service jobs to outsourcing service providers to finish and they do not need to employ service employees in order to improve service performance and reduce salaries expenditure for itself organization office and employees their working environment long term benefits.

Printed by Libri Plureos GmbH in Hamburg,
Germany